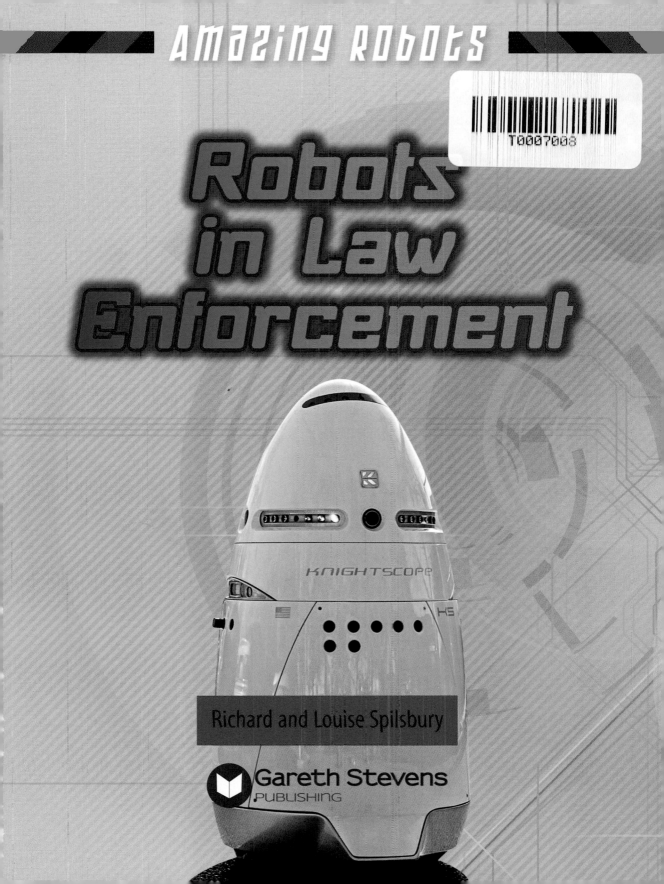

T0007008

Robots in Law Enforcement

KNIGHTSCOPE

K5

Richard and Louise Spilsbury

Gareth Stevens
PUBLISHING

Please visit our website, **www.garethstevens.com**.
For a free color catalog of all our high-quality books,
call toll free 1-800-542-2595 or fax 1-877-542-2596.

Library of Congress Cataloging-in-Publication Data

Spilsbury, Richard.
Robots in law enforcement / by Richard and Louise Spilsbury.
p. cm. — (Amazing robots)
Includes index.
ISBN 978-1-4824-3005-9 (pbk.)
ISBN 978-1-4824-3008-0 (6 pack)
ISBN 978-1-4824-3006-6 (library binding)
1. Robotics — Juvenile literature. 2. Robots, Industrial — Juvenile literature.
3. Materials handling — Safety measures — Automatic control — Juvenile literature.
I. Spilsbury, Richard, 1963-. II. Spilsbury, Louise. III. Title.
TJ211.2 S65 2016
629.8—d23

First Edition

Published in 2016 by
Gareth Stevens Publishing
111 East 14th Street, Suite 349
New York, NY 10003

© 2016 Gareth Stevens Publishing

Produced for Gareth Stevens by Calcium
Editors for Calcium: Sarah Eason and Jennifer Sanderson
Designers: Paul Myerscough and Simon Borrough
Picture researcher: Susannah Jayes

Photo credits: Cover: Photos: Knightscope, Inc. 2014 (www.knightscope.com); Inside:
Blackirobotics: 19; Bozrobot: 39; Dreamstime: Dariusz Kopestynski 21, Photographerlondon
38, Glen Price 13, Stevacer 7, Oleg Zabielin 36; iRobot: 22, 23; Knightscope, Inc. 2014 (www.
knightscope.com): 40, 41; Northrop Grumman Information Systems 6; NTNU/SINTEF: 10, 11;
Robotex: 35, 37; Shutterstock: Albund 16, Bibiphoto 34, Bikeriderlondon 8, Franck Boston
17, Caamalf 4, Steve Estvanik 28, Stefan Holm 14–15, Evren Kalinbacak 9, Meunierd 45,
Neveshkin Nikolay 18, Larry St. Pierre 5, John Roman Images 30, StockPhotosLV 31; Taser
International: 42, 43; US Department of Defense: Airman 1st Class Kristoffer Kaubish 25;
Wikimedia Commons: Digger DTR 27, Gooutside 26, Steve Jurvetson 33, US Department of
Defense/Lance Cpl. Bobby J. Segovia 24.

Printed in the United States of America
CPSIA compliance information: Batch #CS15GS: For further information contact Gareth Stevens, New York, New York at 1-800-542-2595.

Contents

Chapter 1

Robot Cops

In many sci-fi movies and television shows, we see a future world policed by robot law enforcement officers. These future robocops are often humanoid robots—robots designed to look human. In reality, these kinds of robocops and the superhuman powers they use to fight crime are a long way off, but there are many other types of robots already being used in law enforcement today. A robot is a moving machine that can be programmed to perform tasks and gather information from its surroundings. Law enforcement robots come in all sorts of shapes and sizes and are used in a variety of roles, from surveillance in dangerous situations, such as store holdups, to getting up close to and disarming bombs.

The police and other law enforcement officers must keep people safe on the streets and in their homes.

Danger on the Streets

Being a law enforcement officer can be a risky business. Law enforcement officers are trained to protect people from danger, and they often have to put their own lives on the line in order to protect others. They may have to break up fights, stop armed criminals, or chase robbers speeding from the scene of a crime in a stolen car. Law enforcement officers are trained to deal with these situations and have protective equipment to help keep them safe.

Police officers put themselves in harm's way to help other people. Robots can help keep them safer.

Nevertheless, some law enforcement officers are injured or killed in the line of duty. Putting robots in dangerous situations keeps more human police officers safe—robots are easily replaced. Although police officers on television are often shown in high-speed car chases with dangerous criminals, being a police officer is not just about excitement and adventures. Some officers spend a lot of their time on surveillance or patrol missions that can be quite boring. Robots are ideal for this kind of task.

Robots Are the Future

Today, most robots are controlled by human operators, but robots in law enforcement might be able to gather and use specific data more autonomously. This means they could make decisions for themselves. Many people believe that humanoid robots easily could be the future of law enforcement.

Parts of Robots

In order to be useful, law enforcement robots need to be able to move around, they need to be easy and convenient to control, and they need to have parts that can be used to perform different functions. Robots are usually made from a variety of materials, including metals and plastics.

New robots have wheels or tracks that enable them to get to places that older robots could not, such as up stairs.

Control

Many robots are controlled using a computer program. Such programs are very detailed and give commands for the moving parts of the robot to follow. Operators use a screen through which they see what the robot sees and move a joystick, a lot like the joystick you might use for a video game, to control the robot's movement left and right and backward and forward. Most robots are equipped with cameras that feed back live video images of their surroundings so the operator can judge what to do or where next to send the robot.

Moving Parts

Robots move around in different ways, depending on what they are used for and where they will be used. Robots usually have motors and gears that move their wheels or make caterpillar treads turn to move the robot.

Robot arms can have different tools attached to them so that the robot can accomplish different tasks, such as examining potential bombs.

Caterpillar treads, like those on a tank, are made up of a circular belt of ridged metal that moves in a loop over the wheels. These are ideal for robots that are big and heavy, because the treads spread the weight over a large area. Treads like these are also useful because they allow a robot to ride over many different types of land, including rough, icy terrain. Motors and gears also enable the robot grippers or arms to move, twist, grasp, and lift. A robot's moving parts are usually powered by air, water, or electricity.

Sensors

As well as the cameras robots have to film or live stream what is happening around them, robots also have sensors. Sensors are devices that give robots the equivalent of human senses, such as vision, touch, and the ability to feel differences in temperature. Sensors also help robots figure out the size and shape of objects and how much space there is between objects so that they can move around without bumping into things!

There are advantages of using robots instead of humans. Robots are never sick and they do not need to sleep or eat.

Upholding the Law

Robots are used to help law enforcement officers do their job to the best of their ability. There are many different types of robots, and they can be given special attachments or other equipment to carry out specific police jobs.

Capturing Criminals

Imagine encountering a criminal, perhaps with a weapon or being very aggressive. It could be dangerous to get too close. What if a criminal had sneaked into an empty department store at night to steal goods? These are ideal situations for robot security guards. In Japan, a robot has been developed that can fire nets to capture criminals. The robot can move at 6 miles per hour (10 km/h) and be controlled by a smartphone app. The security guard can see what the robot sees using a video feed from its camera, and the robot has sensors to detect any movements in the dark.

Robots can help law enforcement officers catch criminals.

Robot Dozer

Robot dozers are automated bulldozers that can be directed to clear obstacles from roads, for example, if rioters turn over vehicles or set cars on fire to block a street. These obstacles can prevent law enforcement officers from ensuring the safety of citizens in the affected area. Large robotic tracked vehicles, such as ACER, can carry heavy metal blades in front of them to push obstacles out of the way. These robots can also be equipped with gripping arms to grab debris and pull it from a road. Large cutters can be used remove parts of heavier objects or barriers.

Water cannons are sometimes used to control rioting crowds that could harm themselves and others.

Robots Are the Future

Robot Water Cannon

A water cannon is a machine that can shoot out a powerful and high-speed stream of water over a distance of many yards. Robots with water cannons can be guided by remote control to positions where they can be used to spray crowds of protestors or people rioting with water in order to make them move away. Using robots to position the water cannon allows operators to stay a safe distance away.

Search and Rescue

Some police robots are designed to find and rescue victims and police officers from dangerous situations. These situations may include a building that is badly damaged after a disaster, making it unsafe to enter, or a police officer who is injured in a gunfight but cannot move or be rescued by fellow officers because weapons are still being fired. This is when search-and-rescue robots come in handy. They can find and rescue the person in trouble, without getting hurt themselves.

Finding Victims

Snakebots are one type of robot being developed to locate victims. These robots are made up of many different sections so that they are capable of bending and twisting in a number of directions. This allows them to cross rough and cluttered terrain easily. Rubber grippers on Snakebot's underside ensure that it has a good grip and can slither its way through the rubble in collapsed buildings, tiny holes, and narrow spaces such as pipes. These bots can change their shape easily so they can even climb trees and stairs. They are battery-powered and controlled by a remote-control joystick. Snakebots have lights and a camera at the front to help the operator see what the robots see.

Snakebots can slither and move around like real snakes.

Snakebots can save lives. If a building collapses, these bots can get to small spaces where humans and rescue dogs cannot go.

Snakebots also have a two-way microphone and speaker so that the operator can talk to victims to reassure them and to get information about what medical assistance they need. Snakebots speed up rescue operations and reduce the risks to both rescue workers and survivors.

CueBot

CueBot was developed in Japan to rescue earthquake victims. These larger robots use sensors and cameras to locate trapped people and when they have found a victim, they use their robot grippers to lift and carefully load them onto a cart before carrying them to safety. CueBot can also protect police officers under fire as it pulls them to safety by making sure its large metal surface provides a barrier between the danger and the person.

Robots Are the Future

Engineers at the National Aeronautics and Space Administration (NASA) are developing an intelligent robot snake. They hope that in the future, the Snakebot could help them explore other worlds and do building jobs in space, which are impossible for human astronauts to do.

Chapter 2

Surveillance

Surveillance, which is the careful watching of a place or a suspected criminal, is a vital part of law enforcement. By watching or studying what suspects do or a place where criminal activities might be taking place, police officers can build up a picture of what crimes are being committed and gather evidence that can lead to the arrest of suspects.

Different Kinds of Surveillance

Police officers conduct different kinds of surveillance. They may follow suspects by foot, bicycle, or car. In a stakeout, police officers hide in one position and watch a building day and night. Officers involved in surveillance must be careful not to be seen, especially when on the move. New surveillance drones can move and follow criminals and their vehicles, and since they fly in the air, suspects are less likely to see them. The other advantage of drones is that they are always quiet and do not need to stop to go to the bathroom or take a coffee break!

Drones

Drones are about the size of a suitcase or smaller, and can be transported easily in the trunk of a police vehicle. When needed, these unmanned aerial vehicles (UAVs) can be assembled and launched into the air within seconds.

Police officers fly the drone over the area where a suspect is and can watch live images of what they are doing on a mobile computer screen. The images that the drone's camera sends back can also provide officers with potentially life-saving information, such as showing them if a suspect is carrying a gun and in which hand they are holding it, or if other criminals are hiding nearby, waiting to ambush the police.

As well as following suspects, drones can also land on a solid platform with their cameras pointing toward a building or venue, allowing the operator to film hours of video footage while staying safely hidden. As well as an onboard camera, many drone devices also have thermal imaging technology. This technology senses heat given off by the human body and can help officers locate people in the dark or who are hiding among bushes or trees, for example, and then direct foot patrols to the suspect's location.

Many surveillance drones have four sets of blades to help them fly and keep steady in the air.

How UAVs Work

Most law enforcement UAVs are multicopters that can hover in the sky. This means they have several—usually four—spinning propellers or sets of two blades. These are mounted on a frame that also supports a battery and any camera or other sensor the UAV is designed to carry. Shock-absorbing feet allow the drone to land without banging into the ground.

Controlled Motion

In a multicopter UAV each propeller spins in the opposite direction as the propellers on its right and left. It spins in the same direction as the propeller diagonally opposite to it. They control their motion in a fairly simple way, by speeding up or slowing down one or more of the rotors. Speeding up the rotation pushes more air downward, providing more lift for the UAV. Slowing down the rotation reduces lift. Here are examples of how the propeller speeds are adjusted to make the UAV move in different ways:

▶ Hover. All propellers spin at the same speed.
▶ Rise or fall. All propellers go equally faster or slower.
▶ Forward. Speeds up the two rear motors and slows down the two forward ones.
▶ Turn left. Speeds up two propellers diagonally opposite each other and slows down the other two.

Operation

UAV propellers are operated by battery-powered motors. Operators on the ground use a remote control to control the motors. However, a UAV has a built-in computer called a flight

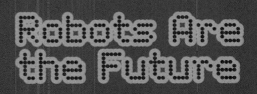

Drones are designed to be easy to use and simple to fly, so that the operators do not need a lot of training to use them.

controller, too, which can adjust the motor speed automatically to stay in the air, for example, if there are gusts of wind. The controller uses data from onboard devices, such as gyroscopes and accelerometers, to adjust the drone's position. These devices, which are also found in many smartphones, estimate the UAV's position and angle in the air. If the operator's instruction to the UAV is to stay hovering, then the controller makes the motors speed up or slow down to keep the drone in one place.

Robots Are the Future

In the future, UAVs may have sophisticated onboard controllers, which allow them to fly autonomously without an operator controlling them. They may also use swarm technology. This allows one operator to control many networked drones at the same time. Together, the swarm of drones can monitor larger areas on the ground than a single remote-controlled drone.

CCTV stands for closed-circuit television. Using a normal television, you see video feed transmitted from cameras through a station, broadcast to an unlimited group of viewers. Using CCTV, the video is transmitted from the cameras to screens seen by only a few. CCTV is widely used for video surveillance by law enforcement officers. They may watch what is happening in a crowd of sports fans, travelers at an airport terminal, shoppers on a street, or in many other places.

CCTV cameras are usually placed high up so that they give operators a good view of an area.

Types of CCTV

CCTV cameras can be mounted in a variety of places, such as on building walls or high towers. Some cameras are always fixed in the position in which they are mounted, but others are pan-tilt-zoom (PTZ) cameras. These cameras give an all-around view because they can move around, up and down, and the camera lens can zoom in or out. Operators in a surveillance room use remote-control systems to monitor the view. Motors move the camera and these may contain special gears so that the feed remains free from shake and judder. By using PTZ cameras, operators can also track a person in a crowd without losing them. Some cameras can film in the dark or through fog. Like night vision scopes, they detect infrared radiation produced by living things. Some CCTV cameras start operating only once sensors attached to them detect motion in a particular space.

Identification

It is very time-consuming and tiring to watch video feed from one or several CCTV cameras on screen. Identifying suspects can be tricky in a crowd of people, and so can seeing if things have been stolen. Robotic technology can help! Video content analysis software searches for changes in shapes, colors, positions, and speed in the images making up a video feed or recordings of a live feed. Facial recognition software automatically identifies people in video sequences that law enforcement officers are looking for. Operators scan images of a suspect into a computer. The software analyzes facial features, such as the shape of the nose or jaw, and how deeply set the eyes are. It then compares these features with those on people in the video, searching for a matching face.

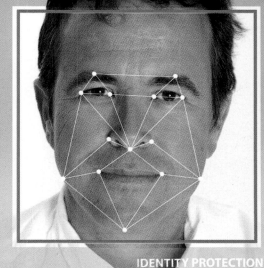

Facial recognition software can be used to match a person's features to a photograph held in a database.

IDENTITY PROTECTION

Name:

Password:

0C000.000.0.00000000.00100111

Robots Are the Future

In the future, facial recognition software used with high-definition images from powerful cameras may be able to detect skin texture including lines, wrinkles, freckles, and moles.

17

On the Ground

UAVs and CCTV cameras have limitations. Drones cannot fly into buildings or through small spaces without damaging their propellers or crashing. CCTV cameras have fixed positions, and they cannot see around corners. This is why law enforcement officers use cameras mounted on small wheeled vehicles, called unmanned ground vehicles (UGVs), too.

Operators can use Xbox controllers to control Landshark UGVs.

Micro UGVs

UGVs for surveillance are usually small, fast vehicles with four wheels or caterpillar treads. They are designed to travel under obstacles and over uneven terrain without toppling over. For example, the xTERRA UGV is about 14 inches (35.5 cm) long and 14.5 inches (36.8 cm) wide with a ground clearance of 1.5 inches (4 cm). It is highly maneuverable and can turn on a dime to reverse or change direction using four motorized wheels. It can move at more than 4 miles per hour (6.5 kph) and up or down slopes of 37 degrees. xTERRA has a battery that lasts for two hours and it also has built-in high-definition cameras, one on the front and one on top. xTERRA's remote control has a range of 0.6 mile (1 km). It can be stored in a case that also houses the monitor and control pad for operating the robot.

Larger Surveillance UGV

A larger UGV, called Landshark, is even more rugged. It weighs 513 pounds (232 kg) and has six wheels. The front two wheels are bigger than the other four so that Landshark can get a grip on slopes and other obstacles. Landshark moves faster and has a much longer battery life than xTERRA. It can carry a range of tools including thermal imaging cameras and sonar equipment for spotting the distant movement of objects. The Landshark has sophisticated equipment to accurately show its position at all times. It also has a surprising ability: it can carry a smaller UGV, which can move through tighter spots that the Landshark cannot squeeze into! This robot is designed to be easily linked to a wide variety of surveillance computers and controlled by readily available Xbox controllers.

Autonomous UGVs can recognize obstacles seen through their cameras and alter their course to avoid them.

UGVs can operate without human control. They follow pre-programmed routes by using computers to compare their position on the ground to GPS satellites in space.

Chapter 3
Bomb Disposal

Explosives are one of the most dangerous threats facing law enforcement officers. Bombs are potential killers and can easily cause life-threatening or life-altering injuries, such as loss of limbs or sight. This is why robots have almost completely taken over from humans in the area of bomb disposal.

The types of robots that can deal with bombs are not cheap to make, but their cost is next to nothing compared with that of a human life.

Humans vs. Robot Bomb Disposal

The traditional way of dealing with bombs was for bomb-disposal personnel to try to make them safe. This meant wearing protective clothing such as heavy body armor and masks, and then approaching the bomb. By very careful handling, some explosives could be dismantled and any detonation device made safe. This often involved cutting wires of the right color and in the right order. It required great skill and knowledge about how the bomb was constructed. This was highly dangerous work. However, today, robot technology has changed all this. Law enforcement bomb squads have teams of robots to get close to bombs while the people remain at a safe distance, out of harm's way.

Robot Bomb Disposal

The usual robot method is for a UGV to drive slowly up to the bomb site. Operators use video feed and other sensors to locate and view the bomb. They will then decide on the best way to deal with the specific explosive device. Bomb-disposal teams generally use the robot to remove the bomb and transport it to a special container where it can be detonated. This is designed to contain the blast without allowing damage to the surroundings. Sometimes robots disarm the bomb and at other times, especially if the detonation device is too tricky to disarm, they may let the bomb explode in a safe place.

An exploding bomb is highly destructive but the toughest robots can survive multiple blasts.

The First Bomb Robots

Bomb-disposal robots were invented in the 1970s for use by British defense personnel during the conflict in Northern Ireland. This was partly because there were multiple casualties from roadside bombs, which were improvised explosive devices (IEDs), instead of standard bombs. One bomb could be very different from the next, so even experienced bomb-disposal experts might not have known how to make the bomb safe.

Bomb-disposal robots are equipped with a wide range of devices to help them detect explosives and bombs. For example, they have cameras so that operators can see the bomb, microphones to hear ticking sounds, and even portable x-ray machines. These can allow operators to see inside bombs so they can figure out how they are constructed and how they might be made safe.

Smelling Trouble

Dogs have a great advantage over humans: their sense of smell is hundreds of times more sensitive. This is why, for years, dogs have been used to smell explosives. Trained sniffer dogs can distinguish between ten different types of explosives. However, dogs can get tired or distracted. Bomb-disposal robots are often equipped with electronic devices to smell explosives. They have sensors that can detect minute traces of the chemicals making up explosives in the air around bombs. Some, such as Fido X3 or Ferret, operate by glowing different colors or amounts when they detect particular chemicals. They are very sensitive: Fido can detect one part of explosive chemical in one quadrillion parts of air! Computers compare the chemical signals with a database of bomb smells so that experts can identify which explosive they are dealing with and how much of it there is. Sniffer attachments are mounted on robot arms that can move to locate the source of the explosive smell.

The iRobot is designed for dangerous missions in situations where there is a high risk of coming under attack.

Robots Are the Future

Dirty bombs are explosives containing materials that can cause hazards after they explode. For example, some may contain substances that cause a radiation hazard and others may contain nerve gases or harmful biological weapons, such as anthrax. Robot sensors can detect these hazards, too. For example, Geiger counters can detect the source and level of radioactivity of nuclear materials that may be found in some bombs.

Getting to the Bomb

Many bomb-disposal robots have arms with claw attachments on them, too. These can be used, for example, to open the door of a car where a bomb might be hidden, or to carefully lift a hidden bomb into plain view or to a place where it might be detonated safely. Arms can also have digger attachments to carefully dig soil away around bombs, or even wire cutters to disarm some explosives.

Bomb Destruction

Once a bomb is found, it needs to be safely disposed of, usually by detonation. In some cases, large, remotely operated bulldozers are used to drive into the bomb. In other cases, UGVs carry small explosive charges to set off a larger bomb. This happens only when experts know exactly what type the bomb is and how big an explosion it is likely to produce. In many situations, bombs are of an unknown type and may have been made from drugstore and hardware store components. Their explosive abilities may be unknown. In such cases law enforcement officers need to use a tool that destroys the bomb without detonating it.

This soldier is preparing a robot to detonate a buried explosive device near his camp.

Shaped Charges

UGVs sometimes place a shaped charge next to a bomb. When operators remotely detonate the charge, it creates a spear of molten metal directed at the bomb. This slices through the outer casing of the bomb and shreds the detonation devices and wires inside, so it cannot work properly. The problem with this is that the high temperature of this hot metal can sometimes detonate the bomb.

To prevent this from happening, today's bomb-disposal UGVs often carry a Stingray liquid blade. Stingray uses the power of a controlled explosion to turn 40 ounces (1.1 l) of regular water into a water blade. The shock wave from the blast moves through the water and speeds it up in an instant into a thin blade shape that shoots out of the Stingray. This blade is much stronger and sharper than a regular knife—it can even cut through steel!

Robots Are the Future

In the future, bomb-disposal teams could use robots equipped with lasers to help them in their work. Lasers can already be used to detect tiny traces of explosive chemicals, for example, traces left on door handles or other surfaces, which give a clue about possible bombs nearby. Prototypes of high-power lasers for destroying bombs are already being tested. These beams of energy will be fired from up to 820 feet (250 m) away to melt the contents of the bombs.

Robots can destroy bombs without putting any human lives at risk.

Land Mines

Land mines are a problem in places where armed conflicts have happened in the past. They are hidden explosive devices designed to detonate when people step on them. Land mines can remain able to explode years after being placed underground, long after conflicts are over. There are probably more than 100 million land mines worldwide and each year, they hurt or kill about 4,000 people.

In some places rats are used to sniff out land mines to keep humans out of danger.

Locating and Clearing Mines

Law enforcement teams may be used to locate and clear land mines. Such officers wear thick protective clothing and find mines using metal detectors or with the help of dogs and rats. Rats find the mines but because they are much lighter than dogs, they do not trigger explosions. Officers may use UGV robots equipped with detectors to locate and destroy individual mines. However, sometimes whole areas are dangerous minefields, and it is very time-consuming to search for and find each mine. This is where demining robots are used.

10.5

Mine Chewer

The Digger is a brute of a robot. It is the size of a small tank with heavy-duty caterpillar treads, and covered with hard steel armor plates. At the front is a spinning 6-foot (1.8 m) roller, studded with tungsten teeth. The Digger moves slowly forward over a minefield with the teeth chewing up the ground to a depth of 10 inches (25 cm) in front of it. Every time a tooth hits a mine, the mine explodes, but even a 16-pound (8 kg) anti-tank mine has no impact on the tough Digger. It weighs in at nearly 13 tons (12 mt), so blasts have little impact on it. The robot is protected by a thick, steel hood over the roller. Steel plates are welded into a v-shape at the front so the blast is directed around the robot. The Digger can clear up to 10,000 square feet (929 sq m) in one hour. It is controlled by operators using a remote control and is designed to be repaired and maintained easily, even by people who have not had special training.

Plastic bombs are hard to detect, so mine-clearing teams use radar systems on UGVs to spot objects underground.

Chapter 4

Traffic Enforcement

Traffic officers are law enforcement officers responsible for directing traffic on public roads and highways. Their role includes enforcing the laws of the road, such as making sure drivers stay within speed limits and stay out of prohibited zones. They are often first responders at road traffic accidents, coordinating the responses of emergency services, establishing causes of accidents, and making sure obstructions are cleared quickly.

Human officers are vital at the scene of an accident, they can help people in ways that robots cannot.

Eyes and Ears

Expert human assistance is vital at accidents and to sort out some road problems. However, some roles of traffic cops are increasingly performed by robots. The reason is that there are only so many traffic enforcers, but millions of drivers on thousands of different roads. Robots can be the eyes and ears of law enforcement officers when they are not physically present.

Traffic Robocops

In Kinshasa, Democratic Republic of Congo, there are two humanoid robots standing 8 feet (2.4 m) tall at two busy interchanges. Normally cops would have to spend long hours blowing whistles and using hand signals to regulate the flow of traffic and allow pedestrians to cross roads safely. In Kinshasa, the robots bend or raise their arms to slow or wave on vehicles. They also have red and green lights to stop traffic from different directions. They are even programmed to speak and tell people when to cross the road.

Identifying Lawbreakers

Most robots traffic enforcers are not humanoid. Some automatically detect the identification of drivers breaking laws. TrafficCapture cameras are special cameras that take photographs of vehicle license plates. They are triggered automatically, for example, when vehicles drive through yellow or red traffic lights or enter zones of roads designed to be used only by public transportation. Sensors such as radar or hidden electrical circuits in the road detect an illegal movement and trigger the camera. Images or video feed from the cameras are automatically compared to computer databases that enforcers can use to match plates with drivers. They can even set up the robots so that cameras look out for particular license plates of wanted criminals.

Speed Limits

Speeding is dangerous to all road users. In the United States alone, speeding kills around 28 people per day, which is more than 10,000 per year. At high speeds, drivers have far less control, braking takes longer, and mistakes can easily happen. This is why a major part of traffic enforcement is identifying those who speed and fining them to ensure they do not repeat the offense.

Traffic officers use speed guns to catch motorists who drive too fast.

Speed Checks

Law enforcement officers use speed guns to monitor vehicles going too fast. Many speed guns work using radar. The gun fires radio waves toward a vehicle and the waves bounce back in an echo. Radio waves move at a constant speed, so the radar system uses the time lag between sending and receiving radio waves to calculate the distance to the vehicle. The shape of the radio wave sent out and the one received can be compared to calculate the speed of the vehicle, too. This is possible when the radar system is mounted in a fixed position or in a moving police vehicle. Increasing numbers of robot speed cameras now work using light rather than radio waves. They use hundreds of pulses of laser light per second to calculate many distance measurements.

Computer systems use this data to calculate the change in distance to an automobile from one second to the next, or its speed. The laser systems have built-in cameras that take photographs of vehicles and when one is speeding, the system automatically uses license plate recognition software to identify the vehicles breaking the law.

Some speed limit robots are sets of two or more mounted cameras a fixed distance apart. If the time taken to move between the two cameras is too small, the driver is speeding.

Hidden Detectors

Some speed limit enforcement robots are partly hidden in the road. Several strips of sensors are embedded at an exact distance apart—often 3 feet (1 m)—in the asphalt, at right angles to the direction of the movement of traffic. The sensors are piezoelectric, which means they produce an electrical signal when they are pressed or change shape slightly. The movement of vehicles over each strip produces a signal and the time interval between the strips is used to calculate speed. This system can also identify the type of vehicle based on its weight, as a heavy truck would create a bigger signal than a motorcycle.

Robot Highways

In 2014 in Oss, the Netherlands, a new kind of highway opened for use. This highway has no streetlights but instead is lit up by the road surface itself. It has green lines along the edges of the highway and the dashed lines in the center glow in the dark.

Smart highway paint stores daylight energy then releases the energy as a glow when it is dark.

Smart Highways

Using glow paint rather than street lights to illuminate highways saves energy. There are many other features planned for highways that will make them smart and able react to different conditions and road users:

▶ **Temperature-sensitive paint.** When the road gets very cold and ice is a risk, symbols of snowflakes or different colors appear in the asphalt to warn drivers that the road could be slippery.

▶ **Interactive light.** Sensors spot approaching vehicles and use power to turn on lights or signs only when they will be useful for the driver. The signs could be used to warn individual drivers that they are speeding.

▶ **Electric lanes.** Wires in the asphalt of particular lanes of highways will allow electric cars to automatically recharge as they are moving.

Robot Automobiles

Many vehicles already have many smart features, such as windshield wipers that turn on when rain hits the glass. One way to make road use safer is to let cars control themselves so that drivers do not have the chance to make mistakes, go too fast, or run red lights. Google Cars have no steering wheel or

The Google Car can drive itself, read road signs, change lanes to overtake, and even stop in an emergency if necessary.

controls other than a large emergency "stop" button. Passengers summon the car by smartphone with instructions on where they want to go, then sit inside and let the car take over. A Google Car uses GPS, cameras, radar and laser sensors, as well as software linked to very accurate digital maps, to know its location and what to expect on the road, such as curves, intersections, and traffic lights. The software allows the car's computers to recognize hazards, such as cyclists, and safely avoid them. Google Car technology has been tested on normal cars on journeys totaling thousands of miles, with drivers on board, ready to take over in case anything goes wrong.

Chapter 5

SWAT Bots

SWAT stands for Special Weapons and Tactics, and SWAT teams are a special branch of the law enforcement service. SWAT teams were first set up in the late 1960s after some incidents of civilians and police officers being shot by snipers. SWAT teams are small groups of police officers trained to use special weapons and tactics to deal with unusual and difficult attacks.

Dangerous Criminals

SWAT teams are called out to deal with criminals who have dangerous weapons and pose a threat to civilians and police officers, to rescue hostages, catch terrorists, and enter armored or barricaded buildings. SWAT teams are trained to crash through barricades, get into buildings and other areas, and capture a suspect with speed and force before the suspect has a chance to injure or kill hostages, officers, or themselves. To help the SWAT team with its work, members are trained to use special weapons, such as submachine guns, assault rifles, sniper rifles, and stun grenades. They wear heavy body armor, including bulletproof helmets and vests to protect themselves from attack, and they carry shields that can withstand gunfire. To get into barricaded buildings they have special tools and armored vehicles, which they can drive through gates or walls.

SWAT teams are trained to deal with highly dangerous situations, such as terrorist attacks.

Robots like this AVATAR can help SWAT teams achieve their missions and save lives.

Assessing the Problem

The first job a SWAT team does when arriving at an incident is to assess the situation and decide what action to take. For example, they find out all they can about the suspect and the layout of the area in which they are working. Possibly the most important part of this is pinpointing exactly where suspects and hostages are inside a building or other area. To do this, SWAT teams may use equipment such as night vision goggles, which help them see in the dark, or motion detectors, which tell them when someone is moving around.

Increasingly, SWAT teams are also using robots to help them with their important law enforcement work. Reconnaissance robots, such as AVATAR (see page 37), help SWAT teams by allowing them to inspect dangerous situations. By sending in robots to check an area, human members of the team do not have to risk their lives doing so. Knowing exactly where armed suspects are also limits the risks of officers being injured or killed when they launch their assault.

Recon Robots

SWAT teams can be called out at any time and end up anywhere, so it is vital that any robots they use for reconnaissance, or recon, are small and portable, or easy to carry around. SWAT teams also need robots that are easy to assemble and use at a moment's notice, and that are able to move across different types of surface and can be operated from a safe distance.

Throwbots

Recon robots are used as cameras to provide information for officers before they enter an unknown or dangerous situation. Most SWAT robots have some type of vision system, such as video feed cameras, night vision, or thermal imaging cameras, which they use to send back live images of their surroundings. The advantages of robots called Throwbots are not only that they are small and simple to use, but also that they can easily be thrown into an area, through which they then move quietly. They send back live video streams showing where things such as doors, corridors, and rooms are, and where barricaded suspects and hostages are hidden.

Throwbots can tell SWAT teams where suspects are so that they can get them in their line of sight.

AVATAR

One type of recon robot, AVATAR, is controlled by a handset and by using its caterpillar treads, it can move quickly and easily across almost any type of surface, including stairs, sand, clothing, grass, and ice. It is waterproof and it can even flip itself back up if it is knocked over. AVATAR has two-way audio, which means the operator can hear what is going on where the robot is and also speak to hostages or suspects via the robot. It also means operators can use them to distract suspects and provide cover for SWAT team members. AVATAR has high-powered LED lights to light up dark corners and a 360-degree camera that shows the operator a view of everything going on around the robot. Equipment, such as cameras, can be plugged in to the basic robot for different missions. Several AVATARS can be used at the same time to gather intelligence for a major incident or one that is happening over a large area.

Operators command K9s—dogs trained to help SWAT teams—through AVATAR'S speakers.

AVATAR robots help SWAT teams quickly and safely inspect dangerous situations.

Ground Assault

When SWAT teams have assessed a situation, they may decide to storm a building to capture the suspects and free any hostages. The problem is that suspects often barricade themselves in well-protected buildings with tough metal gates, or they may block roads with overturned vehicles. It can take several SWAT team members a long time to break into such buildings or clear vehicles, and all the time they are working, they are putting themselves at risk of being fired at by the suspects. This is why heavy-duty robots such as BOZ-1 can help with this part of a SWAT mission, too.

When SWAT teams storm a building, they are vulnerable to attack from inside.

BOZ-1

The BOZ-1 robot is a large, heavy robot that SWAT teams use to help them clear a path and enter buildings. It has five cameras and is controlled using a laptop and joystick. It has a long robotic arm with a hydraulic jaw at the end that can tear, crush, drag, and lift vehicles or demolish bricks, metal, and wood to break through doors, gates, and walls and allow SWAT team members to get inside.

A hydraulic machine is one that is operated by pushing liquids or gases through a pipe. This creates a large pressure, or pushing force, that can be used to move a piston (a cylindrical piece of metal) up and down. This in turn moves the BOZ's cutting jaws closer together or farther apart, making them open and close. The jaws can grip a metal gate, which the robot can then pull back, tearing the gate apart. The jaws can also grip large objects, such as cars, so the robot can drag them out of the way.

BOZ robots combine brute force with arm tools that can lift and grip precisely.

BOZ-1 can drag vehicles up to about 3,300 pounds (1,500 kg) in weight!

Amazing Arm

BOZ-1 can extend its arm up to 11 feet (3.5 m) high. The arm can also be used to help with reconnaissance. For example, it can be used to punch open car trunks or doors and look inside with its three infrared and two zoom cameras, showing the operators what is inside. BOZ-1 also has six main wheels and four extra wheels that it can use when necessary to cross particularly rough ground, making it pretty unstoppable!

Chapter 6

Street Beats

In movies, we often see law enforcement officers in high-speed car chases or tackling dangerous criminals. In reality, life for an average police officer is not just about excitement and adventure. Most police officers spend a lot of their working day patrolling the streets. They walk, ride, or drive around an area or at an event, such as a festival or baseball game, keeping an eye out for signs of criminal activity, getting to know people in the local community, and making those people feel safe. Now companies are developing robots and other robot equipment to help police on patrol.

Dalek or Robocop?

The Knightscope K5 robot stands about 5 feet (1.5 m) tall, weighs 300 pounds (136 kg), and looks a little like a Dalek from the television show *Doctor Who* as it cruises along at about 3 miles per hour (4.8 kph). The K5 is equipped with a variety of sensors including cameras, thermal imaging sensors, microphones, a license plate and facial recognition detector, and a sensor that can measure temperature, air pressure, and carbon dioxide levels in the environment. It uses these measurements to detect any unusual levels of noise, air,

K5 can roam around autonomously for 24 hours before it needs to be recharged.

or temperature change and it can compare the data it collects with government files. It can alert officers to come to the scene and make enquiries or an arrest.

Self Defense

K5 does not carry weapons but it can defend itself. If someone stops in front of it, the robot moves around that person, sending live film of them to its control center. If the person tries to stop the robot from doing its job, the robot beeps to warn them to step back and if they do not, it lets off an ear-piercing alarm that alerts the control center. The control center sends an officer to see what is happening and to warn the person to stop interfering with the robot. People in trouble can press a button on the robot to speak to an officer, ask a question, report a crime, or to ask for help.

Robots Are the Future

Currently, K5 is being tested at just a few sites. The hope is that in the future it will be used instead of police and security guards to patrol a variety of places including office buildings, malls, neighborhoods, and campuses.

At the Ready

Could the next step in robotic law enforcement be humanoid police officers? Some law enforcement officers already use robotic equipment to improve their policing, from cameras worn on sunglasses that can record live footage to the high-tech equipment they wear on their utility belts. These high-tech pieces of equipment are starting to give law enforcement officers robotic powers and are helping them investigate crimes and solve cases.

AXON Flex is such a small video system that no one would ever know it is attached to this officer's sunglasses.

In the Line of Sight

A device called AXON Flex is a very small video system that police officers can attach to their sunglasses, collar, helmet, jacket, body, or the dashboard of a vehicle. The camera records video footage from the officer's perspective and can record clear images even in low light, showing exactly what the officer's eyes see, even after dark. The video footage can be used to provide evidence of a crime and to show exactly what happened at an incident and avoid false complaints about bad police treatment, for example. If an incident is being recorded, police officers are more likely to maintain their high standards. The device also automatically uploads reports onto a website, saving officers from having to do this at the end of every working day. That means they can spend more time on patrol and protecting people on the street.

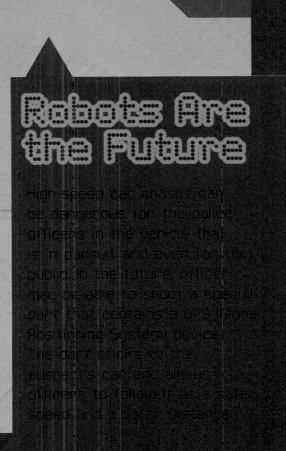

Linking data from robotic equipment with a patrol car computer ensures that officers have the latest updates about a crime.

Shot Sensors

In parts of a city where guns are fired fairly often, police officers can also use a system of several carefully positioned electronic sensors that record when and where a weapon is fired. This is very useful in areas where witnesses are scarce or may be unwilling or too scared to tell police where criminals were shooting from. The information collected by the sensors is also beamed immediately to police computers in patrol cars, so that officers can get to the scene quicker than usual. This could mean that they could reach a shooting incident in time to stop it escalating and perhaps keep people from being killed.

Robots Are the Future

High-speed car chases can be dangerous for the police officers in the vehicle that is in pursuit and even for the public. In the future, officers may be able to shoot a special dart that contains a GPS (Global Positioning System) device. The dart sticks to the suspect's car and allows officers to follow it at a safer speed and a safer distance.

43

The Future

At the moment, law enforcement services use a combination of humans and robots, with human operators always in control of the robot systems. This gives police officers the ability to use their experience and judgment about how best to deal with a situation, while using a robot unit for surveillance, reconnaissance, patrol, or defusing bombs. However, inventors are coming up with new technological ideas all the time and many people believe that in the not-too-distant future, we may see humanoid robot officers policing our streets!

Here Comes HAL

HAL stands for Hybrid Assistive Limb, and HAL is a robotic exoskeleton suit. Humans can wear it to support their movement and to give them superhuman strength to lift weights. It gives a human robotic powers. It is powered by a battery pack and has sensors that tell the robot suit how the body is starting to move. It reads the signals sent by the human muscles to interpret what the wearer intends to do and then the robot uses its motors to help it and the human body inside it move or achieve what it wants, such as lifting a very heavy weight.

Exoskeletons like HAL could be used by police officers for protection and to increase their strength. Already robots have been equipped with a Taser™ stun gun to stop people who are carrying a gun and will not surrender. It seems a logical next step for humanoid-style robots to be invented that could take on the role of an officer and make the arrest, too. Do you think this could be the future of law enforcement?

What will the future of law enforcement be? Will human or humanoid police officers protect us?

Robots Are the Future

Could there be problems with robot police officers? Some people fear that even when we have the technology to build an autonomous police force, we will need to consider other issues before putting them on the streets. What if a police robot has weapons and shoots the wrong person by mistake? There are concerns that when people are involved, we will always need human police officers because only they can understand and really assess what another human being is likely to do or is capable of.

Glossary

accelerometers devices that measure the speed at which something is moving

autonomously acting on its own, without outside control

biological weapons germs, such as anthrax, used as weapons to kill or harm people

caterpillar treads metal bands that move around the wheels of a vehicle to help it move across rough or uneven ground

civilians people who are not in the police or military

detonation the action of causing a bomb or explosive device to explode

drones robot aircraft

evidence documents, witness reports, and other information that can prove whether something is true or false

exoskeleton suit a rigid external covering for the body

first responders the people who are first at the scene of an accident or other emergency

gears parts of a machine that help control its speed

Geiger counters instruments used to detect and measure radiation

GPS GPS stands for Global Positioning System, a system of satellites that work together to give people exact locations on Earth

gyroscopes devices that are used to determine direction

high-definition cameras cameras that record very high-quality video

humanoid like a human

hydraulic using the pushing force of liquid under pressure to do work

improvised explosive devices (IEDs) homemade bombs made and detonated in ways that are different from conventional military weapons

infrared rays of light that cannot be seen

laser a very narrow beam of highly concentrated light

maneuverable able to move skillfully and quickly

motors machines that make things move

night vision describes devices that help us see at night

patrol keep watch over an area

portable able to be moved or carried around

prototypes the first working models of a new invention

radar a device that sends out radio waves for finding out the position and speed of a moving object

radiation a type of dangerous and powerful energy

radio waves invisible waves used for sending signals through the air

reconnaissance the act of studying or watching a place or enemy to find out information about them

remote control operating a machine from a distance

rioters a large crowd of people behaving in an angry and uncontrolled way, usually as a protest

sensors devices that sense things such as heat or movement

sniper a person who shoots at people from a hidden place

software a computer program that is developed to do a specific task

sonar a system that uses sound waves to find and calculate the location, size, and movement of underwater objects

stakeout a situation in which police secretly watch a place where there may be criminal activity

surveillance keeping watch on or observing someone or something

suspect a person thought to be guilty of a crime or offense

Taser a weapon that fires barbs, which give an electric shock

terrain land or ground

thermal imaging describes a device that makes images of things we cannot see by sensing the heat they give off

tungsten a hard metal that can be used to make thin wire

x-ray invisible rays of light that can pass through objects to see inside them

For More Information

Books

Ceceri, Kathy, and Sam Carbaugh. *Robotics: Discover the Science and Technology of the Future with 20 Projects* (Build It Yourself). White River Junction, VT: Nomad Press, 2012.

Clay, Kathryn. *Robots in Risky Jobs: On the Battlefield and Beyond* (The World of Robots). North Mankato, MN: Capstone Press, 2014.

Furstinger, Nancy. *Helper Robots* (Lightning Bolt Books). Minneapolis, MN: Lerner Publications, 2014.

Leider, Rick Allen. *Robots: Explore the World of Robots and How They Work for Us* (The Fact Atlas Series). New York, NY: Sky Pony Press, 2015.

Shulman, Mark. *TIME For Kids Explorers: Robots.* New York, NY: Time For Kids, 2014.

Websites

Find out more about how police robots work at:
science.howstuffworks.com/police-robot.htm

There is a brief history of robots at:
http://idahoptv.org/sciencetrek/topics/robots/facts.cfm

This site provides an interesting introduction to robotics:
http://www.galileo.org/robotics/intro.html

Index